# Teddy

# the Ghost Dog
of Red Rocks

by
**Jerilynn Henrikson**

Rowe Publishing

Softcover ISBN 13: 978-1-939054-23-4 • ISBN 10: 1-939054-23-0
Hardcover ISBN 10: 978-1-939054-24-1 • ISBN 10: 1-939054-24-9

Interior illustrations by Deborah Cotterman.

Chapter heading photos courtesy of the William Allen White
Family. Used by permission.

Red Rocks cover photo courtesy of Red Rock Photography and
Jennifer Baldwin. Used by permission.

Period post card of the Mit-Way Hotel by Eckdall & McCarty Book
Store, Emporia, printed in Germany, 1920.

At the time of this book's publication, all facts and figures cited are
the most current available.

3 5 7 9 8 6 4 2

Printed in the United States of America
Published by

Rowe Publishing
www.rowepub.com
Stockton, Kansas

*For school children everywhere:*
*may you always find joy*
*in learning.*

# Contents

*President Teddy Roosevelt and Teddy the dog share a relaxing moment on the porch at Red Rocks in 1912.*

# A Ghost Dog

My name is Teddy, and I am a ghost. Before I became a ghost, I was a small white fox terrier dog with dark, expressive eyes and perky brown ears. I was not the ideal fox terrier because of my short nose. And whoever docked my wagger chopped it to a stub instead of leaving a four or five inch tail. I guess you could say I was short-changed on both ends. But I was handsome, cheerful, mostly obedient, and well-loved by my family.

As Teddy the Ghost Dog, I now find myself eager to tell my story, for my ghost-self has insights and thoughts beyond the understanding of my dog-self. For example, as a dog, I was smart enough to understand many words in human speech, words like "sit," "stay," "come," "food," to name a few. But now as a ghost dog, I understand human perfectly. I have been a presence here at Red Rocks for more than a hundred years, and my long history in this house gives me much to say.

I belonged to the family of William Allen White, a famous newspaper editor from Emporia, Kansas. Many called him Will. His newspaper, *The Emporia Gazette*, has been in the White family now for four generations. I spent my living years with Will, his wife Sallie, and their children Bill and Mary in the big red stone house known as Red Rocks at the corner of 10th and Exchange Street in Emporia, Kansas. All of them but Mary outlived me, but I am the one who remains.

Will bought me for his children in 1911. He paid five dollars for me and picked me from a litter of five because I boldly trotted up to him and tugged his pant leg. "That one is a troublemaker," the man who owned my parents warned.

"I like to stir up a bit of trouble myself sometimes," answered Will with a broad grin.

I was named after a great friend of Will's, President Theodore Roosevelt, the 29th president of the United States. Naming me for President Roosevelt was a terrific idea. TR already had a toy bear named for him because he rescued a bear cub on one of his hunting expeditions. I, on the other hand, was named for Teddy because the two of us had so much in common. The American Kennel Club (AKC), a group of dog experts who determine the preferred characteristics of show dogs, states that a smooth fox terrier by nature is bold, intelligent, athletic, friendly, loyal, and determined, also an apt description of TR. President Roosevelt visited us several times at Red Rocks because he found a political ally in Will, and also great food at Sallie's table, engaging children, stimulating conversation, and a handsome dog. TR also found that the citizens of Emporia had enough sense to leave him in peace to rest and relax. Many famous people came to Red Rocks, but TR was always my favorite visitor. That man really knew how to scratch a dog's ears.

I especially remember one of President Roosevelt's visits not long after I came into my family. I made it my business from the first to always be a part of whatever was happening. TR loved Sallie's fried chicken and had put in an order for some at Sunday dinner after church. Martha the housekeeper, Mary, Bill, and I had stayed behind to set the table and prepare the side dishes.

Sallie's golden, crispy chicken was keeping warm on a huge ironstone platter in the oven. We heard feet on the porch, and Martha reached into the oven to slide out the platter of chicken, but she lost her grip on the heavy platter; it slipped to an angle, and all the chicken slid onto the floor. Martha, Bill, and Mary gasped in horror. I grabbed a drumstick and ran with it up the back stairs. Martha began piling chicken back onto the platter and told the children, "I scrubbed this floor this morning, and if either of you says a word about this, you are double Dutch done for!" TR ate four pieces. I found my drumstick, bone and all, to be delicious.

On another visit, President Roosevelt, Will, Sallie, Bill, Mary, and I were relaxing on the porch when I decided it was time for a game of fetch. The conversation had begun to lag, so I trotted across the lawn and picked up a good sized branch that the wind had blown from the oak tree. I had to struggle a bit to find a grip right in the middle so I could balance that twisty branch without dragging it on the ground. Bill laughed and told TR, "Look, Mr. President. You're not the only one who knows how to carry a big stick." (You see, President Roosevelt had once described dealing with enemy nations with these words, "Speak softly, and carry a big stick.")

The AKC also advises that fox terriers make good family dogs if, "properly trained and given

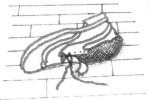

plenty of exercise for body and mind." We terriers can get into big trouble if we get bored. Will muttered, "blasted dog" when he found I had chewed one of his favorite shoes. A snappy dresser, Will had just bought those soft gray leather dress shoes to match his new pearl-gray suit. Grandmother White, who lived next door, was not a happy granny when I ruined all her petunias by digging for moles. She shooed me out of her yard with a broom. And another time, it took days for Sallie to forgive me for shredding a Chinese silk feather pillow that sat on the sofa. Do you know how many feathers there are in a big sofa pillow? And how much fun it is to scatter them all over the living room? I must admit, I became a master at looking heartsick and ashamed, even if I really wasn't. It's also hard to look innocent with feathers stuck to your lips.

*Sallie and Will in a typical moment of affection.*

# 2

# The Sage of Emporia

What a team Will and Sallie were. They collaborated on several books, and Sallie read, commented on, and approved most of Will's editorials. Early on, Sallie spent much time at the newspaper office writing articles and editing copy. They were a loving couple, and this love was the foundation of the White family of Red Rocks. Later, when the children were small, Sallie spent most of her days at home with Bill, Mary, and me.

Every morning the weather per-
mitted, Will walked the eight or nine
blocks to the *Gazette* office. And on
those mornings Sallie and I often walked with him as far as
the corner. There Will would
lean his briefcase against a big
elm tree in the parking, take Sallie
into his arms, and plant a kiss firmly
on her lips. I would circle them joyfully, and he
would give me a pat. Then he would lean down,
scoop up his briefcase and march off to work. This
warm relationship was the heart of the home Will
and Sallie made for their children and me, that
lucky little fox terrier.

Sallie loved to tell the story of how Will wrote
the editorial that made him famous. Bill and Mary,
even I, Teddy the dog, loved to hear her tell this
tale:

One morning, as he approached the
*Gazette* office, Will encountered a bunch of
men in overalls waiting for him in front of
the office. Will was hurrying to finish his
work early to catch a train to join Sallie
in Colorado where she was recuperating
from a recent illness. Will, as always, wore
a three-piece suit, dress shirt, and tie.
Short and portly, he nonetheless moved
with jaunty self-assurance, even giving
these men one of his broad smiles. One

of the characters stepped in front of him, halting Will in his tracks. The rest quickly surrounded him. Pushing and shoving, they began to jostle him rudely. They were shouting insults such as:

"That rag of a paper of yours is full of progressive garbage."

"Why don't you get off your high horse?"

"You dress like a store manikin."

"How come you let that String Town trash into your house?"

"Who do you think you are, Shorty?"

One ruffian rudely punctuated his insults by poking Will in his round stomach with a walking stick. (If I had been there, that man, sure as Sunday, would have had a fresh hole in the seat of his overalls.) Will was so angry he could not muster a reply. Pushing them aside, he hurried to his office where he sat down at his desk and began pounding furiously on his stiff-keyed little Underwood typewriter. The editorial he wrote that day became his hallmark, titled "What's the Matter With Kansas?" In this rowdy crowd, Will saw a lack of respect for education, business sense, intelligence, and leadership that he thought plagued Kansas and explained the loss of population and capital from the state he loved. Later, Will began to worry that he had been too angry when he wrote that editorial.

He told his wife when he joined her at the Colorado cabin, "Sallie dear, I'm afraid I have made a serious mistake. I wrote an editorial after an encounter with some knuckleheads that accosted me on my way to the *Gazette* before I left town. They were so ignorant and so rude, and I was so angry. I wish I had waited to let you read it."

Later, after she had read the published editorial, she said, "Yes, you were certainly angry, but a little righteous indignation is sometimes called for. I think you said exactly what needed to be said. I just hope the people who most need to hear it are listening! Sometimes cooling down is overrated," she added, patting his hand affectionately.

"What's the Matter With Kansas?" after appearing in the *Gazette* was picked up by other papers across the nation and made Will famous. Sallie always told this story with pride. Will became known as "The Sage of Emporia," won two Pulitzer Prizes for his excellent writing, appeared twice on the cover of *Time* magazine, and was a respected advisor to several Presidents. Sallie kept extra copies of the magazines in a desk drawer. After his death, the U.S. Postal Service honored Will by putting his image on a three-cent stamp. Sallie treasured these and many other mementoes. I hope she felt my presence watching as she occasionally sorted through them, touching, smiling, and remembering.

Yes, the feisty spirit that TR and I shared was also a part of William Allen White's character. Will's editorials showed his courage. During the first years of the 1900s, the Ku Klux Klan was active in Kansas, even in peaceful little Emporia. They spoke hateful words about Catholics, Jews, recent immigrants, and the folks living in String Town and they frightened dogs and children with their scary hoods and midnight torch-lit rallies and marches. Will wouldn't have any of it. He hated the injustice, prejudice, and cowardly secrecy, and he exposed members whenever he got the chance by naming them openly in the *Gazette*. One morning the *Gazette* staff found a noose hanging from a light post in front of the building: one of the clan's favorite methods of intimidation.

Once when the organization scheduled a statewide meeting at the Broadview Hotel in

Emporia, Will called and got a list of registrants and published the list in his newspaper. Some local klansmen decided to protest by marching past Red Rocks in robes and hoods. Mary opened the door and told me, "Sic 'em, Teddy." I ran out barking and growling. Then I recognized the man who came to clean the stable by his smelly boots and ran up to say hello. When he bent over to shoo me away, his hood fell off. We both made a grab for it resulting in a fierce tug-of-war. "Let go you stupid mutt," he hollered. He won most of the hood, but I got away with a respectably sized mouthful: another coward unmasked.

This cartoon featured Will during his run for governor of Kansas in 1924. I always felt the cartoonist should have pictured Will carrying a rolled up *Gazette* rather than a gun. Words were always his weapon of choice. I know I got swatted with a rolled up paper on occasion.

One dark night in the early 1920s, I awoke to the flash of dancing flames reflected on the walls. After a quick look out the pantry window, I charged, barking up the stairs, to rouse Will and Sallie. The children awoke too and we all rushed to open the front door to find a large cross burning on the lawn of Red Rocks: another Klan protest? Everyone thought so. Years later a columnist for the *Gazette* confessed that he and some of his fraternity brothers had planted the cross as a prank. They must have known this was a serious lapse in judgment. The confession came a half-century after the event.

*A posed photo still conveys the warmth between a dad and his children.*

# 3

# My Life at Red Rocks

The house known as Red Rocks remains at the corner of 10th and Exchange, and so do I. I am a presence here among the furniture and fixtures. The rugs and pillows, the books and bookcases, the windows and staircases remain much the same as the day I died in 1923.

Red Rocks is a State Historic Site now. There are history-loving volunteers called docents, who come to dust and take curious groups through the house. Visitors ask questions about William, Sallie, Bill, and Mary. They want to know about the china and the dining room table, Sallie's favorite recipes, and where the old helmet and framed fans came from. Visitors sit in Will's upstairs study and marvel at his old typewriter as the docent explains the pictures on the walls. One picture shows Will sitting next to the brilliant scientist, Albert Einstein, in a group photo of those receiving honorary doctorate degrees at the Harvard graduation of 1935. Guests like to hear about the Presidents and other famous visitors who came to enjoy talk with Will and share our small town life.

Folks from the community schedule special events at Red Rocks now. Young couples have weddings in the garden, and the site director schedules special tea parties. Ghost dogs do not eat, but I love the smell of lemon bars (and remember the taste), and the ladies all look so elegant in their flowered dresses, hats, and gloves.

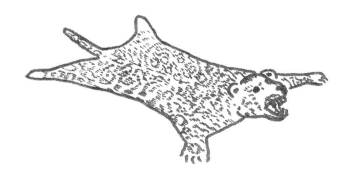

Touring school kids are fascinated by the jaguar rug in the bedroom at the top of the stairs. This rug was a gift from President Teddy Roosevelt and is one of my favorites too. Even now as Teddy the Ghost Dog, I love to sleep there. Back in the 1950s, Will and Sallie's granddaughter, Barbara White Walker was being courted by her future husband, David Walker, who spent the night in the house while visiting in Emporia. He slept in the bedroom at the head of the stairs. Late that night I trotted up the stairs, my ghostly toenails ticking on the wooden steps, and into the bedroom, where I plopped onto the rug. David was awakened and was astounded when he turned on the light, and nothing was there.

Officials from the Kansas State Historical Society are quite concerned about the jaguar rug. It is beginning to show its age: hair loss and loose claws. I hope they don't blame me. I must tell you, I am determined to continue sleeping there. I refuse to believe my ghostly form can hurt the rug. I admit though that sometimes I turn around three or four times before I curl up for a nap.

Back when I was a pup, in the interest of my mental and physical health and to protect shoes, flowers, and furniture, Bill and Mary were put in charge of making sure I got plenty of exercise. In addition to tug-of-war, Bill and I loved to play tag. When Bill chased, I would tuck my tail end under me and scamper and dart in circles and figure eights. When I chased, I would give Bill a good head start because I was so much faster. Sometimes he would climb a tree or hide under the mock orange bushes. I could always find him and bark him out of the tree or flush him from the bushes. Then he would roll with me in the grass and laugh. He would tickle my belly and I would lick his face.

Mary's favorite game was "water wars." This could be played outdoors or in. She would "hunt" me down and blast me with her squirt gun. I really loved this game. I would turn and face her and catch the squirts in my mouth, snapping and growling at the streams of water. Sometimes she included other family members in the game. Sallie would pretend to be angry when Mary ambushed her from behind a chair or the staircase, but the game always ended in hugs and laughter. Will often kept a full water pistol in his pocket, and would give Mary as good as he got. He was really handy with that pistol, and Mary would squeal and run when he got her right on the nose.

One day, the game escalated into all-out war: children and dog, Sallie and Will. It began with Mary shouting at Bill, "Stand and fight, you coward. Stop hiding under the table!"

When Bill came scrambling from beneath the table, pistol blasting, Sallie insisted, "Outside, you two."

Will, grinning his biggest grin teased, "Now mother, they're just having a bit of fun." Then he produced a small squirt gun from his jacket pocket and brazenly showered the front of her dress. At this point, I began barking sharply and Sally drew a turkey baster from a kitchen drawer, filled it at the sink, and soaked me thoroughly. Then Will doused Bill with a fruit jar full of water from the sink. Will called a truce when all were dripping wet and weak with laughter, and I had barked myself hoarse. The family changed into dry clothes. I shook hard, one of those traveling doggy shakes, starting with the ears and rippling to the tail and made another puddle on the kitchen floor. Sallie wiped up the mess with an old towel, and we all had ice cream on the porch.

I loved them all, but I was the children's dog. Bill was always eager for a chase through the house, or a game of fetch in the back garden. I was sad for days when he went off to Boston, Massachusetts, to attend Harvard. Mary would sometimes let me follow when she went horseback riding. Her love of riding and daredevil antics on horseback were a worry for Sallie, but in those early, carefree days, she and I shared joyous adventures on the open prairie.

Fox terriers and horses are a natural combination from the tradition of the British foxhunt. Even though Mary rode a flat, English saddle, she did not have a red hunt coat, and I never spotted a fox, but there were birds to flush and rabbits to chase and the joyful freedom of the open prairie.

Mary and I also shared an ornery sense of fun. She always laughed at my jokes. Especially the one when I scared the neighbor's orange cat, Oscar, as he was staring at his reflection in the garden lily pond. He jumped into the water. There really is nothing funnier than a wet cat. My stumpy ghost dog tail still wags when I remember soggy old Oscar shaking his wet paws and high stepping all the way down the alley.

When everyone else in the house was busy, I was pretty good at finding my own entertainment. I loved to take my rubber ball to the top of the stairs and drop it down the staircase. Bong, bong, bong, bump, bump, rollllll. I would run after it, then race with it again to the top of the stairs to repeat the process. I could usually get in three or four rounds of this game before Sallie got sick of the noise, took the ball away, and tossed it into the kitchen sink. Another of my tricks was to stalk Martha, the housekeeper. She always cleaned with amazing concentration, humming as she dusted or scrubbed. I would pad softly up behind her, give a sharp "YAP," watch her jump, and run like crazy.

She would say, "Drat you, Teddy" through clenched teeth, and throw her dust rag at me.

*The Mit-Way Hotel was one of the jewels of*
*Commercial Street.*

# 4

# I Keep Busy

When the children were at school, I could always go outside to bark at squirrels, dig for moles, harass Oscar, or hunt mice in the stable. Sometimes I just went exploring. In those days, there were no leash laws. The house rule for the family dog stated that I was to be in by dark. It was only a few blocks to Commercial, the main street of Emporia, where I would loiter in front of Morris Drug Store, hoping for the last bite of someone's sandwich or the end of an ice cream cone. The Mit-Way Hotel was always a place of interest. The pool hall there attracted a "spotted clientele" as Sallie was fond of saying. I didn't go inside, but the entrance breathed out tobacco smoke, and much of the language that sailed past the door was pretty salty.

If I chose to travel east, the wide prairie lay just a block or two away, sprawling toward the sunrise. I loved chasing birds, especially killdeer. They do an impressive broken wing act to lure dogs and people away from their nests, typically laying their eggs on a patch of bare ground or gravel. I knew I would never catch the fluttering bird, but for a terrier, the chase is its own best reward.

I might also go next door to check on grandmother. Will's mother, Mary Hatten White, lived in a handsome foursquare house she had built, right next door to Red Rocks. She was a down-to-earth woman, the best kind of grandmother. Bill, Mary, and I loved her without condition, and she loved us right back. She adored hugging her grandchildren and often invited me into her lap when she sat rocking on her porch and watching passersby on Exchange Street.

Grandmother set an example of the value of hard work. When Will was a boy in Eldorado,

Kansas, she had run a small hotel, including doing all the cooking for guests who wanted meals. If Sallie was busy, grandmother often came with dinner, bringing fried chicken or pot roast across the garden to Red Rocks, and she also watched the children and me whenever she was needed. We could be a challenging trio. Once we all pounded up her front steps following Mary across the porch, through the open front door, and into the parlor. Problem was, Mary was on horseback! "CHARGE!" she yelled. I think we were re-enacting Teddy Roosevelt and the Rough Rider's cavalry charge in the battle of San Juan Hill.

Surely the family also inherited Grandmother White's ideas about racial tolerance. As a young teacher in Council Grove, Kansas, she had pressed her determination to open her classroom to children of any race, even winning a court decision supporting her stand.

Back in the 1920s, Emporia really was a small town. East Street marked the east edge of town, and West Street marked the west edge. The Kansas Normal School, now Emporia State University, and the Neosho River were at the north end, and Soden's Grove and the Cottonwood River lay at the south end of town. A trolley traveled from East Street

to West Street. The tracks ran down the middle of 12th Avenue, where they turned south to run down the middle of Commercial Street to the Grove. Yes it was a small town, but covering it from north to south, or east to west was a goodly trip for a short-legged dog.

Even though Red Rocks has stayed much the same, the town has not. Emporia is three or four times bigger than it was back when I lived for my twelve years from 1911 to 1923. My energetic spirit sees many changes: no trolley, no Morris Drug Store, no Mit-Way Hotel, no roaming dogs. From Red Rocks, I would have to travel three miles east, or five miles west to reach the grass-lands. There don't seem to be leash laws for ghost dogs, but even so, these days I feel obliged to stick close to home. My heart is here, and it is my job to keep watch.

Red Rocks was a lively place back then. Sallie and Will loved visitors, parties, dinners, delicious food, and lively conversation. Drop-ins were al-ways welcome. "Pull up a chair," Sallie would command. A favorite expression of hers was, "We like to fit them in with a shoe horn."

As youngsters, Bill and Mary had many friends too, and the big old house welcomed them all. The Whites had shelves and stacks of books through-out the house and were eager to share them with friends and neighbors including colored neigh-bors from nearby String Town. Mary loved the out-of-doors, but she also loved to read. Will bragged that she had read all the works of Twain, Dickens and Kipling before she was ten: not just *Tom Sawyer, Oliver Twist,* and the *Just So Stories,* but all of these writers' works. I always rejoiced, yapping and running circles when there was a crowd. I loved the energy young ones brought to the house, and they shared cookies and sandwich crusts with me whenever I begged.

Holidays at Red Rocks were celebrated much the same as in other homes in Emporia. The Christmas spirit came with carols at church, oranges, nuts, and small treasures stuffed into stockings, popcorn and cranberry trimmed trees, early morning presents from Santa, and belt-stretching turkey feasts. And, of course, a special bone from the butcher for me.

Will and I liked Thanksgiving best because both of us loved food. Sallie and Martha brought out the good china, silverware, crystal, and linens to set a lovely table. All the leaves were added and the big table nearly filled the dining room. Even so, family and friends were "shoe horned" in, elbow to elbow. Platters heaped with ham, roast beef, and turkey, bowls brimming with mashed potatoes, gravy, dressing, candied sweet potatoes, peas, creamed corn, and fruity salads, and dishes filled with olives, pickles, and pickled beets crowded every inch of the dining room sideboard and kitchen and pantry counters. I would lurk beneath the table and watch for a friendly hand to offer me a bit of turkey, or a hunk of homemade roll. Then came the pies: pumpkin, of course, and apple, mince, and pecan. And if someone didn't like pie, there was always a plate of lemon bars.

In the years after Will's death, Sallie and the current housekeeper, Bertha, would invite neighborhood Halloween trick-or-treaters in for lemon bars, homemade fudge, or juicy polished apples. As a ghost myself, I especially enjoyed the white sheet with eyeholes costumes. A brother and sister duo I enjoyed watching walk past from their house on Union Street on their way to school came several years for treats. The boy was dark haired and round faced, and his older sister, ponytail bobbing, seemed confidently in charge. "I know this big old house is kind of scary," the girl told her little brother. "But the lemon bars are worth it. And Halloween is supposed to be scary." Come Halloween I still love to sit in the pantry window and watch the little ghoulies parade up and down 10th Street.

*Sallie often worried about Mary when she went riding.*

# 5

# "I Don't Want to
# Grow Up"

Allof us loved Mary. Her father saw great
potential in her to continue his work at the
*Gazette.* As a high school junior, she was assistant
editor of the school yearbook and in line to be
editor her senior year. She was also beginning to
show some talent as a cartoonist and was proud
that some of her drawings had been used in the

annual. Later others were included in the 1921 Kansas Normal School annual. Sadly William's hopes for Mary were not to come true.

One sunny spring afternoon after a challenging day at school, Mary decided to take a relaxing horseback ride. The new prairie grass beckoned, dazzling freshly green. She was heading north on Merchant Street when she turned to wave to a friend. She had her hat in one hand and the reins in the other. As she waved with her rein hand, she pulled the loping horse into the parking, and her head hit the overhanging branch of a tree. She slipped stunned from the saddle and crumpled to the ground, never really to regain consciousness. She died three days later.

Expressing the hurt our family felt is beyond the words of a little ghost dog. Will however, wrote a powerful editorial about Mary and her death. The day following the funeral, he and Sallie went to his office at the *Gazette*, closed the door, which was not their habit, and together as always, produced what became Will's most remembered piece of writing. I can only imagine the tears that fell as they faced life without their child.

They described Mary saying, "She was mischievous without malice, as full of faults as an old shoe. No angel was Mary White, but an easy girl to live with, for she never nursed a grouch five minutes in her life." They also spoke of Mary's independence: remembering how she had decided

to join the Congregational Church without inform-
ing them; recalling how she refused to wear fancy
clothes and insisted on keeping her long hair in
a simple braid; mentioning her sense of fairness
and concern for the poor; picturing her driving
carloads of kids, colored and white, all over town;
calling her a Peter Pan who claimed she never
wanted to grow up. How tragic that her words
came true. Will ended the piece with a moving
description of the final moments of her funeral.
"A rift in the clouds in a gray day threw a shaft of
sunlight upon her coffin as her nervous, energetic
little body sank to its last sleep. But the soul of her,
the glowing, gorgeous, fervent soul of her, surely
was flaming in eager joy upon some other dawn."
As a lasting tribute to her, the White family purchased a large tract of land in south Emporia to be
used as a park by all the citizens of Emporia. It is
named Peter Pan Park.

Red Rocks became a house of mourning. A few
days after the funeral, Bill and his Harvard friends

returned to Boston and their classes. The big old house echoed with emptiness. Will and Sallie leaned upon each other. I tried to be a steady, sympathetic companion by keeping close and offering a nudge or a paw. Visitors came with kindness, food, and encouraging words, but only time could make us better...not well, but better. For parents, there is no forgetting the loss of a child. Missing Mary must have been especially hard for Bill. He was isolated from the rest of us away at school, and the death of his beloved sister brought the full weight of his parents' expectations onto his shoulders.

As a dog, I just could not understand where Mary had gone. I searched upstairs and down, hunted through the stable and under the mock orange shrubs, and slept at the foot of Mary's bed. I found less joy in chasing Oscar, and I took longer and longer naps. As my living self, I never really understood that our Mary was not coming home.

As months and years passed, Will's round face began to find its smile again, but for the rest of his life, there were times when a certain sadness seemed to cloud his expression.

One day I dropped my ball at Sallie's feet as she sat quietly in a wicker rocker on the wide porch. Absent-mindedly, she picked the ball up and tossed it into the yard. She smiled when I bounded after it, and she laughed and hugged me when I returned and dropped the ball into her lap. She was returning to herself, but the death of her precious girl would mark her until the end of her days.

Since Sallie's death in 1950, my ghost-self has missed her presence in the house. But a large, lovely oil painting of her hangs above the landing on the staircase. I often sit quietly looking up, staring at her pretty face and remembering her strong, gentle spirit. Not long ago, the portrait was taken down to be cleaned. I was happy and relieved when, after several weeks, it was returned to its rightful place above the stairs. I stretched up to see Sallie's newly brightened face and softly touched the bottom of the frame with my paws. Somehow the painting came off the wall and fell onto the post where the stairs turn. The post tore a sizeable hole in the canvas.

I was afraid I might have triggered the accident with my paws. The portrait was taken away again to be fixed, has been returned, and the repair is skillfully done. I still spend many hours looking up at Sallie, but I will not be touching the portrait ever again. After it fell, I hid under the mock orange bushes for two weeks. I guess even as a ghost, a terrier can still be trouble.

*Will and Teddy at Red Rocks not long before Teddy died in 1923.*

# 6

# I Am Lost and
# I Am Found

O n April 23, 1923, the *Gazette* posted the
following editorial by William Allen White.

## Lost

A dog—a little white fox terrier with liver-colored ears and dark, intelligent eyes; an oldish dog as dogs go, being past twelve, and slow moving, a bit deaf and maybe not so clear-sighted as he was once when two little children used to tumble him over the grass at his home ten years ago. He has always been a good moral dog, and if he had his love affairs and romantic adventures, he was always in by nine o'clock. But now he has been gone two days. Possibly he has been crippled in an accident; it is also possible that he is sick, and it is barely possible that he may have gone to a home where there are children, though such perfidy seems unlikely. But at any rate, any one who knows of such a dog who left home Sunday morning will please call up phone 28 and tell the news, be it good or bad, to an anxious family to whom the little dog is a living link to a happy and beautiful past.

Then on April 28, Will posted another editorial.

### Found

For five days the *Gazette* telephone has been ringing to tell the editor of people who thought they had found his little lost dog. It seems to have been raining white fox terriers of a certain age with stumped tails and yellow ears in and around Emporia. But none of the dogs described over the phone was the real lost dog except one—and he was the dog we long had sought and mourned because we found him not. C.W. Jacobs found him yesterday morning ten miles east of town just north of the Sixth Avenue road. The dog was lying on a wisp of hay in the road, starved and sad and footsore. How he had come there no one knows; whether he had followed off wine, women or song, or had been kidnapped by people who turned him loose when they realized what an old dog he was—that no one can say. But the Jacobs family took him, gave him food and a place behind the kitchen stove, and phoned to his people.

> From all over the country letters and
> telegrams have come in response to
> the notice that this little dog was lost.
> Nothing in the world excepting a child
> will draw people together in sympathy
> as will the love of dogs.

Well, here is the story. That Sunday morning
Sallie and Will left for church. I was lonely and
felt a familiar ache in my heart urging me to find
Mary. That fine spring day reminded me sorely of
the day Mary had left home and never returned.
In my experience, when she went riding, she usually headed east into the prairie, so that is where
I went. I trotted along as dogs do, sniffing and exploring. The bluestem grass grows terrier belly
high in late April and lush as a lawn. I found a cov-
ey of bobwhite quail and chased them until they
flushed in a grand whirrr. A meadowlark piped
his gold-throated tune from a fence post. Lazy
white clouds drifted in the wide blue sky.

I almost stepped on a cottontail rabbit. It had
probably heard me snuffling along and flattened
to the ground hoping I wouldn't spot it. It bolted
and I gave chase, dashing this way and that. The
critter dove into a hole with me right behind. The
burrow narrowed, and I was nearly stuck, but I
managed to back up to a place where the burrow
was wide enough for me to turn around. Whew,

I panted, tongue lolling. In my younger days, I'd have had that rascal.

Then I worked my way down a shallow draw and came upon a Hereford cow and her newborn calf. The cow saw me and stared. She came toward me, and I barked sharply at her. She charged. This surprised me, as did her speed. She caught me with her left horn and tossed me about fifteen feet. I landed headfirst, hit a good-sized piece of limestone, and was knocked nearly senseless.

Luckily, the blow knocked the wind out of me and stopped my barking. The cow no longer saw me as a threat and withdrew. Dazed and disoriented, I curled up in the soft grass and dozed off and on until morning. My head hurt. I felt like I'd been run over by a cow. I found some rainwater in a draw and had a drink; then I found myself wishing I had caught that tricky cottontail or one of those quail.

Disoriented and confused, I really was not
sure which way would lead me home, so I headed
toward a road I could see topping a far distant hill.
My progress was slow because I was stiff and sore
from the cow attack. I limped along the road until
I found some hay that had blown from a passing
hay wagon; there I lay down for a rest. I made
this hay nest my base for several days, making little trips, limping up and down the road, looking
for food. I found the carcass of a rabbit that had
been hit by a car and chewed the hide and bones.
Fortunately the April rains had left pockets of water in the road ditches.

A few cars passed, but no one stopped until
Mr. Jacobs found me, took me to his house, fed me,
and called Will to come retrieve me. I am sure you
can imagine how happy I was to see Will and Sallie
and go home to Red Rocks. There were wags, and
licks and kisses and tears. I never strayed far from
home again and never will, but this adventure
cost me dearly. Perhaps there were injuries from
the cow encounter, or maybe a bone splinter from
the rabbit carcass had harmed my stomach. About
two weeks after my return, I felt ill and went into
the back yard to find a shady spot for a nap under
the mock orange bushes. When I woke up, I was a
ghost.

Will and Sallie were painfully sad to find my
little dead body. They buried me where I died,
under those bushes. I know I was a "link to that

happy and beautiful past" that Will referred to. But as you now know, I never really left them. I hope they felt my presence and were comforted by it. After a long battle with cancer, Will died in 1944. Bertha the housekeeper at that time claimed she saw my ghost-self jump onto his bed as he passed. Sallie died in 1950, Bill in 1973. My hope is they all share with Mary that beautiful distant other dawn Will spoke of so eloquently in the editorial about her death.

*Father and son share a conversation.*

# 7

# The Second William

After Mary died, Will and Sallie's hopes for the future of the *Gazette*, turned toward Bill. He became a journalist and went overseas to cover World War II, even broadcasting via radio from war torn Finland on Christmas of 1940. I remember sitting with Will and Sallie in front of the tall radio, as my ghostly self cocked an ear toward the sound of Bill's voice. After the war, a promising

 career with CBS radio was beginning to take shape. But Will's health was failing. On Bill's rare visits home, even a ghost dog could see that he was unhappy. He spent hours on the phone to contacts in New York. But in spite of all his longings for a career in broadcasting, he made the decision to come back to Emporia and the *Gazette*.

An accomplished writer, William Lindsay White continued the tradition of excellence at the *Gazette*, even winning awards in page design. He published several books and stories, three of which became successful movies. One of these was a story called "Lost Boundaries" based on true events about a light-skinned colored doctor who was able to pass as white to practice in a white community. Tragically when the truth came out, his white patients rejected him, and the colored community would not accept him either. Sometimes I am convinced that dogs are smarter than people. A dog does not care about skin color, how much money his master has, or what part of town he lives in. A dog just wants kindness, loyalty, pats on the head, games of fetch, drumsticks, and lemon bars.

Another book, *They Were Expendable*, a story about naval battles in the Pacific in WWII, also became a movie starring John Wayne. I'm not sure who John Wayne was. I just know Bertha the housekeeper was really impressed.

When Mary was in high school, she noticed that there was no place for her colored girlfriends to gather to chat and relax, and hounded the administrators at the school to fix the situation. After her death, the board of education approved a lounge for them. Years later, in the spirit of Mary's efforts for equal rights, Bill purchased the privately owned "whites only" Peter Pan Swimming Pool across from the Peter Pan Park and donated it to the city, stipulating that it be open to all Emporians. Mary would have been so proud of her big brother.

Naturally Bill had to deal with comparisons with his father. Some Emporians judged him as aloof, foreign. He had picked up a British accent on his assignments in England. He wore a funny little one-eyed eyeglass called a monocle and expensive tailored suits. He and his wife Kathrine loved New York and the urbane, big city lifestyle and spent six months of each year living there. Sadly, most folks in Emporia did not remember him as I did: the eager, quick-minded boy who loved to throw the ball for his little terrier dog. Sometimes people forget that a person, or a dog, can only be what he is. I hope the conflict with locals did not cause Bill pain. I wish I could have offered him the comfort of a game of tag, or a tumble in the grass. There just wasn't much a ghost dog could do.

Bill's service to Emporia and the *Gazette* did not, however, go unnoticed. In 1973, just before his death from cancer, the Emporia Civic Auditorium was renamed The William Lindsay White Auditorium in his honor. Money from a memorial fund established at his death was used to plant over 300 trees in the city. Even as a spirit, a dog appreciates a well-placed tree. A bust of him and a plaque bearing a sample of his writing are displayed in a park named for him just north of the *Gazette* offices.

*WLW was making a career as a broadcaster for CBS when his father's death brought him to the decision to return to Emporia, his family, and the* Gazette.

*The famous porch at Red Rocks.*

# 8

# A Haunted House

Bill and Kathrine's little girl, a British child they adopted after WWII, grew up to become Barbara White Walker. She and her husband David Walker were the third generation of Whites to own the *Gazette*. Their son, Christopher White Walker and his wife Ashley are the fourth. Their children Grace, Hattie, and Will give me hope that there will be a fifth. I do so love the sound of those three happy children laughing and playing on the staircase when they come to visit Red Rocks.

In 2001, Barbara White Walker, Will and Sallie's granddaughter, donated Red Rocks and its contents to the Kansas State Historical Society. And so the White family home now belongs to all Kansans. It is fitting that Will and Sallie White's mission of sharing their ideas through the *Gazette* and their open door hospitality, is now available to anyone who wants to visit Red Rocks.

As the oldest resident of the house, in addition to telling my story, I make it my duty to eagerly welcome guests to the site. I sit near the door when groups come for tours to greet everyone with a friendly, stub-tailed wag. But it seems that very few of those who come are aware of my presence. There was one little neighbor girl who used to ride her bike down the alley and around the block. One day she looked up and saw me watching her from the pantry window. I know she saw me because she smiled and waved. She reminded me of Mary. Later, she came to tour the house and told the tour guide her story of seeing me in the window.

Early last spring some pleasant ladies asked permission to use the interior of Red Rocks as the backdrop for some photos for a book they had written about quilts and quilting. While they were arranging quilts and cameras, I began barking at a squirrel on the porch. I startled them a little, but they were not afraid. I have a reputation for being friendly, even as a ghost.

Not long ago a group of young fellows from Emporia who call themselves "The Men of Mystery" came to the house with bags of sound equipment and cameras looking for evidence that Red Rocks is haunted. They set up their equipment and spent two, five-hour sessions taping and listening. I followed them through the house, top to bottom, sniffing at their shoes, running past the cameras, yapping at their microphones. The film showed fuzzy green low light shadows. But when they turned up the sound recordings, yes! weak, but distinct barking. Teddy is here!

Lately, a new cat has been poking his nose around Red Rocks. He is a black and white tuxedo cat, which just makes him look overdressed for every event he decides to come to **uninvited**. He belongs to the neighbors across the alley. His name is Hoover, but I think the name comes from a vacuum cleaner, not a President. He often has his nose to the carpet. He slips into the visitor center with folks coming for a tour or the site director when she is working on programs or organizing events. She seems to like him, but I wish he would keep his nosey nose out of my business. He always seems to be searching for something: a mouse, some catnip, a GHOST DOG? I am in charge here. I've tried to bark him away, but he takes great delight in ignoring me. He knows I'm here, and I know he knows I'm here, and he knows I know he knows I know he's here. He is almost as stubborn as a terrier!

Recently the site director and one of the docents were in the house getting things ready for a tour. I tried sitting in front of them, cocking my head this way and that as they discussed how to arrange the chairs. Frustrated because they kept ignoring me, I began to bark. They heard me, but they still were unable to see me. They were so surprised. Their eyes widened and their mouths dropped open. The site director has gotten into the habit of calling out to me when she comes into the house, "Hi Teddy, it's me." I agree with Grandmother White who often said, "Consideration for others is the soul of good manners."

I tell you my story because I think there are lessons in it for all times. The love between wife and husband is passed to their children and from them to following generations. The love a family has for the home is passed to the community and into the larger world. The ideals of love, family, community, tolerance, moderation, learning, generosity, and optimism are the best of what Will, Sallie, Bill, and Mary White shared with each other, their community, their state, their nation, and the world. There was even enough left over to inspire a small terrier dog to remain in the family home to protect the legacy and share the story.

Meanwhile, maybe someday, the director, a docent, or a visitor will see me again. It is not in my nature to give up trying. Still, I will take my work as the remaining resident of Red Rocks seriously. And, ever loyal, I will wait, wait...longing for my family to return. I am a ghost, but after all, I'll always be that spunky, determined little white terrier with brown ears and a stubby tail, Teddy the Ghost Dog of Red Rocks.

# Afterword

If you decide to come for a tour, look, listen, and even if you do not see or hear me, please remember to say a polite, "Hello Teddy, it's me." And if you are inspired by my story of Red Rocks, pass it on to a friend.

Love to all, Teddy.

# Author's Notes

- This story is a blend of history and fiction. The historical material is factual with the following exceptions: The Klan marching past Red Rocks is a fictional incident taken from the made for TV movie, "Mary White." It is not factual, but wouldn't it be fun if it were?
- Details of Teddy within historical incidents are the result of my imagination.
- The "re-enactment of San Juan Hill" refers to the historic charge of Teddy Roosevelt and the Rough Riders in the famous 1998 battle for Cuba in the Spanish American War.
- The incident of Teddy ticking up the staircase was reported by David Walker and Barbara White Walker.
- One of my volunteer "readers" suggested that I might need to explain to my young audience that a "three piece suit" consists of jacket, pants, and a vest.
- After much thought, I chose to use the word "colored" to refer to African Americans as it is the word Will used in the "Mary White" editorial.

- When Mary died, the family was living temporarily at 913 Exchange while Red Rocks was being restored and remodeled following a fire. The family's initial period of mourning would have begun here, but as Red Rocks was Mary's home, for the sake of continuity, I labeled it as the house of mourning.

- I use the term "parking" in the story twice. Another of my readers asked that I explain that the parking is a strip of grass between a sidewalk and the street. Many times shade trees are planted there by the city.

- The story of what happened to Teddy when he was lost is from my imagination except the facts taken from Will's editorial, "Found."

- The incident of Teddy jumping into Will's deathbed is "urban myth."

- The incident of the girl on the bike was related to a docent during a tour by the girl herself as a visitor.

- The burial of Teddy beneath the mock orange is from my imagination: possible but unlikely as his remains would probably have been found when the garden was dug up and replanted in 2005.

- This story is designed to appeal particularly to upper elementary students; however, I hope that anyone who reads it will like it.

- My aim is to make the vocabulary challenging enough to encourage young readers to grab a dictionary or check the internet. I believe that reading makes you smart.

# Sources

"American Kennel Club - Breeds." *American Kennel Club - Breeds.* Web. 3 Dec. 2012. Website

Buller, Beverley Olson., and Monroe Dodd. *From Emporia: The Story of William Allen White.* Kansas City, MO. Print

Buller, Beverley Olson. *A Prairie Peter Pan: The Story of Mary White.* Kansas City, MO: Kansas City Star, 2010. Print.

"Red Rocks." - *Kansas Historical Society.* Web. 23 Jan. 2013.

White, William Allen, and Helen Ogden Mahin. *The Editor and His People;* New York: Macmillan, 1924. Print.

White, William Allen, and Russell Humke Fitzgibbon. *Forty Years on Main Street,* New York: Farrar & Rinehart, 1937. Print.

White, William Allen. *The Autobiography of William Allen White.* New York: Macmillan, 1946. Print.

"William Lindsay White (1900-1973): In the Shadow of His Father [Hardcover]." *William Lindsay White* (1900-1973): In the Shadow of His Father: E. Jay Jernigan: 9780806129020: Amazon.com: Books. Web. 18 Nov. 2012. Website

# Acknowledgments

I owe thanks to many. First to my favorite person, who remains closest to my heart and my computer, my husband, Duane. He has been interested and involved in the entire process, always willing to read the latest draft and offer honest advice. (And as the one closest to me, his criticisms are the hardest to hear, at the same time they are often the most relevant.) My dear friends Sharon Stewart, Jan Traylor, Ann Eldridge, and editor in chief, Sharon Stephens, have been invaluable help with editing and advising about the story's appeal to my young audience. Roger Heineken's thorough knowledge of Emporia and its history have made him a reliable sounding board and advisor. Beverley Buller has offered wise counsel on editing and publishing. June Underwood laid down her paintbrush to read a late draft and give me some valuable suggestions. Chris and Ashley Walker have added enthusiastic support including permission to use photos from the White family collection. Also I offer a special thank you to fifth and sixth grade students at Olpe Elementary School for their excited reaction to Teddy's story. Their positive response to a reading at their school gave me the inspiration to "get it done!" Finally and importantly, thank you to Deborah Cotterman for her lively, engaging illustrations. This has been an enjoyable project, and a journey I could not have taken alone.

# Discussion Questions

- It is an old saying that dogs are like their humans. Which humans in the story are most like Teddy? Explain how this is so.
- Read aloud a sentence or two that you think explains why Teddy remains a presence in the house.
- Can you spot any places in the narrative where you see that the author was influenced by the language Will White used in his editorials? Give examples.
- Read aloud a favorite passage and explain why you like it.
- List four incidents you think are fictional. List four incidents you think are historical facts.
- If you like the book, write a note to the author explaining why. If you don't like it; oh well, can't win 'em all.
- If you REALLY like the book, go to prairiepatchwork.com to see other other works by author, Jerilynn Henrikson.

## Language Arts Upper Elementary Common Core State Standards for *Teddy, the Ghost Dog of Red Rocks*

| Strand | Substrand | CCR Anchor Standards Cluster | Focus of Each Standard (and suggested activity) |
|---|---|---|---|
| Reading | Literature | Key Ideas and Details | 3. List characters introduced in Part 1. |
| | | Craft and Structure | 4. Define and use in a sentence: jostle, muster, hallmark, righteous indignation, sage, feisty, lapse, loiter, rift, fervent, perfidy, urbane. |
| | | Craft and Structure | 5. Group: Create an illustrated timeline of the story's action. |
| | Informational Text | Key Ideas and Details | 1. Group: From library or internet, find a text of "What's the Matter with Kansas." Find some words that show how angry WAW was when he wrote this. Find a current explanation of the editorial to help you explain it to your classmates. |
| | | Craft and Structure | 3. Classify paragraphs as mostly historical, or mostly fictional. |
| Writing | | Text Types and Purpose | 1. Write a review of the book. Support your opinions with specific examples from the story. Look at some professional reviews for examples. |
| | | Research | 7, 8, 9. Write a research paper on a topic suggested by the story that you want to know more about. |

## Language Arts Upper Elementary Common Core State Standards for *Teddy, the Ghost Dog of Red Rocks*

| Strand | Substrand | CCR Anchor Standards Cluster | Focus of Each Standard (and suggested activity) |
|---|---|---|---|
| Speaking and Listening | | Comprehension and Collaboration | 2. Invite a speaker from the White family, the historical society or the author of the story to speak about relevant topics suggested by the book. |
| | | | 3. Write down questions that come up as the speaker talks. Ask your questions. |
| | | | 4. Give a report to your classmates on your research. |
| Language | | Conventions of Standard English | 1, 2. Find examples of the following types of sentences: simple, compound, complex, compound/complex from the text. Use as models to write your own examples of these types of sentences. Review rules of punctuating these sentences and punctuate correctly. |

CPSIA information can be obtained at www.ICGtesting.com
Printed in the USA
LVOW10*1945031014

407234LV00001B/36/P